Beagles
and Other Hounds

Editorial:
Editor in Chief: Paul A. Kobasa
Project Manager: Cassie Mayer
Writer: Marta Segal Block
Researcher: Cheryl Graham
Manager, Contracts & Compliance
  (Rights & Permissions): Loranne K. Shields
Indexer: David Pofelski

Manufacturing/Production/
Graphics and Design:
Director: Carma Fazio
Manufacturing Manager:
  Steven K. Hueppchen
Production/Technology Manager:
  Anne Fritzinger
Manager, Graphics and Design:
  Tom Evans
Coordinator, Design Development
  and Production:
  Brenda B. Tropinski
Cartographer: John Rejba

For information about other World Book publications, visit our website at http://www.worldbookonline.com or call 1-800-WORLDBK (967-5325).

For information about sales to schools and libraries, call 1-800-975-3250 (United States), or 1-800-837-5365 (Canada).

World Book, Inc.
233 N. Michigan Avenue
Chicago, IL 60601
U.S.A.

Library of Congress Cataloging-in-Publication Data

Beagles and other hounds.
    p. cm. -- (World Book's animals of the world)
  Includes index.
  Summary: "An introduction to beagles and other hounds, presented in a highly illustrated, question-and-answer format. Features include fun facts, glossary, resource list, index, and scientific classification list"--Provided by publisher.
  ISBN 978-0-7166-1369-5
  1. Hounds--Juvenile literature. 2. Beagle (Dog breed)--Juvenile literature. I. World Book, Inc.
SF429.H6B43 2010
636.753'7--dc22
                        2009020163

World Book's Animals of the World
Set 6: ISBN: 978-0-7166-1365-7
Printed in China by Leo Paper Products LTD., Heshan, Guangdong
2nd printing August 2011

Picture Acknowledgments: Cover: © Masterfile Corporation; © Robert Daly, Getty Images; © Adriano Bacchella, Nature Picture Library; © Imagemore/Getty Images; © Anna Utekhina, Shutterstock.

© amana images/Alamy Images 17; © Van Hilversum, Alamy Images 19; AP Images 39; © DeAgostini 37; © Dreamstime 15, 31, 43, 49, 51; © Robert Daly, Getty Images 5, 41; © Imagemore/Getty Images 25; © Shannon Stapleton, Reuters/Landov 53; © Masterfile Corporation 7, 27, 61; © Scott Tysick, Masterfile Corporation 33; © Adriano Bacchella, Nature Picture Library 35, 45; © Biosphoto/Peter Arnold, Inc. 59; © Jeff Greenberg, Photo Edit 21; © Shutterstock 3, 4, 23, 29, 47, 55, 57; The Kill (1830), oil on canvas by Henry Thomas Alken (© SuperStock)

Illustrations: WORLD BOOK illustration by Roberta Polfus 13.

Beagles
and Other Hounds

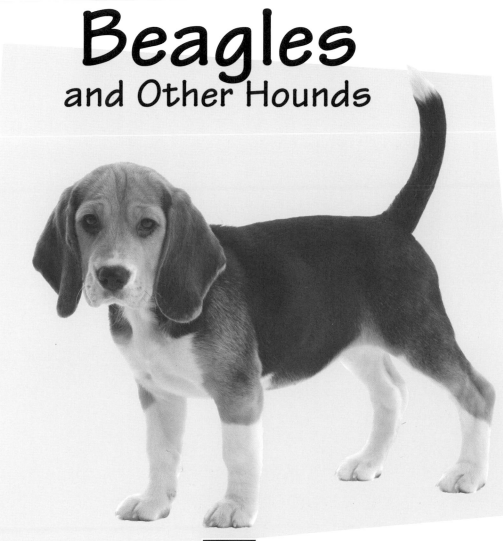

WORLD
BOOK

a Scott Fetzer company
Chicago
www.worldbookonline.com

Contents

What Is a Hound?

Hounds are dogs known for their ability to help people hunt animals. Different breeds of hounds are found all over the world. (A breed is a group of animals that have the same type of ancestors.)

Hounds come in many shapes and sizes. The Rhodesian *(roh DEE zhuhn)* ridgeback, a breed of hound originally from Africa, is a large, fast hound that helps people hunt lions! Other hounds, such as the basset hound, are fairly small and slow.

Hounds are among the oldest known dogs. They were originally bred to be hunters. Some hounds have a very strong sense of smell, which helps them to follow the animals they are hunting. Other hounds have great sight and can run fast. Many hounds make a unique baying or howling sound.

Because hounds were bred to be hunters, they tend to be alert, love the outdoors, and have great endurance. They are considered to be great family pets because of their sweet nature.

6

A beagle

How Did Breeds of Hounds Develop?

Today, most people eat meat that comes from animals raised on a farm. But in the past, people had to hunt animals for their meat.

Hounds are dogs that were bred to be good hunters. Sometimes you can tell what animal a dog was bred to hunt by looking at the dog. For example, dachshunds *(DAHKS hunds)* are a type of hound that were originally bred in Germany in the 1600's to hunt badgers. Their long noses and bodies are good for digging into badger burrows (underground holes). Borzois *(BAWR zoys)* were originally bred in Russia before 1500 to chase and catch wolves. Their strong jaws are capable of holding a struggling animal.

Some hounds use their strong sense of smell to track down animals. These dogs include the foxhound, black and tan coonhound, beagle, bloodhound, basset hound, dachshund, and petit basset griffon vendeen *(puh TEE bah SAY gree FOHN vohn day OHN)*. Other hounds, such as the greyhound, Afghan, borzoi, and Irish wolfhound, hunt using their sight.

Foxhounds hunting

9

When and Where Did the Beagle Breed First Appear?

In England during the 1500's, people often kept packs (groups) of hounds for hunting. Larger hounds hunted deer, while the smaller hounds were used for hunting rabbits. These smaller dogs developed into the beagle breed. They are thought to be the first hounds to hunt by following smells.

Before 1860, there was a small dog in the southern part of the United States known as a beagle. Between the 1860's and the 1890's, English beagles were brought to the United States. These dogs were bred with the existing southern beagles. This created the dogs that people today call the American line of beagles. By the end of the 1800's, this beagle was one of the most popular breeds in North America. In the United Kingdom, the English beagle kept its old blood line.

Today, beagles are still used as hunting dogs, but they are most often bred to be lovable family pets.

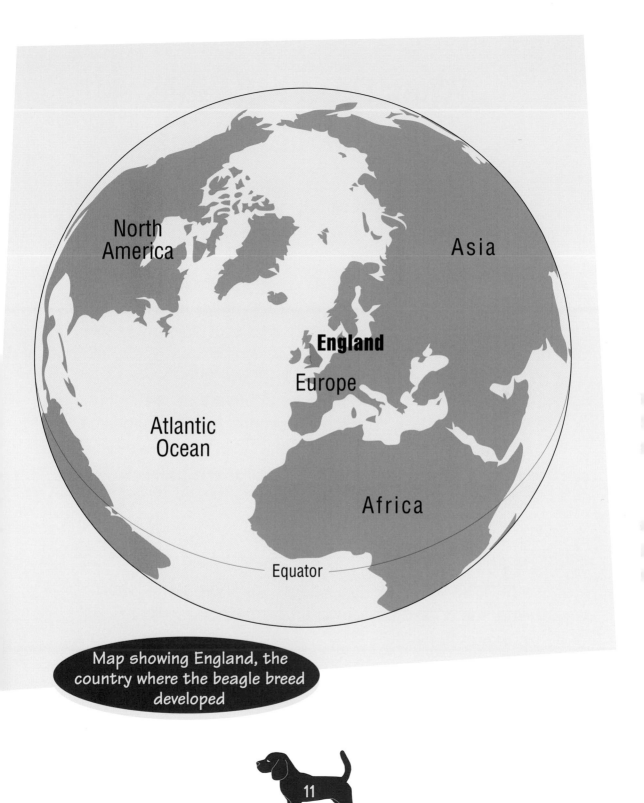

North America

Asia

England

Europe

Atlantic
Ocean

Africa

Equator

Map showing England, the
country where the beagle breed
developed

11

What Does a Beagle Look Like?

Beagles are small, sturdy dogs that weigh between 8 and 30 pounds (8 and 14 kilograms). In the United States, the beagle is bred in two sizes. Larger beagles are from 13 to 15 inches (33 to 38 centimeters) tall at the shoulder. Smaller beagles are up to 13 inches tall.

When you think of a beagle, you probably think of sad eyes and long, floppy ears. These ears are not just cute. They help the beagle hunt. As the beagle walks or runs, its ears flap in the wind. This creates movement that brings smells back to the beagle's long nose.

Beagles come in several different colors. Many beagles are a combination of colors, such as red and white or tan, black, and white. Their hair is short and has a hard, stiff texture. The hair does not feel soft and fluffy.

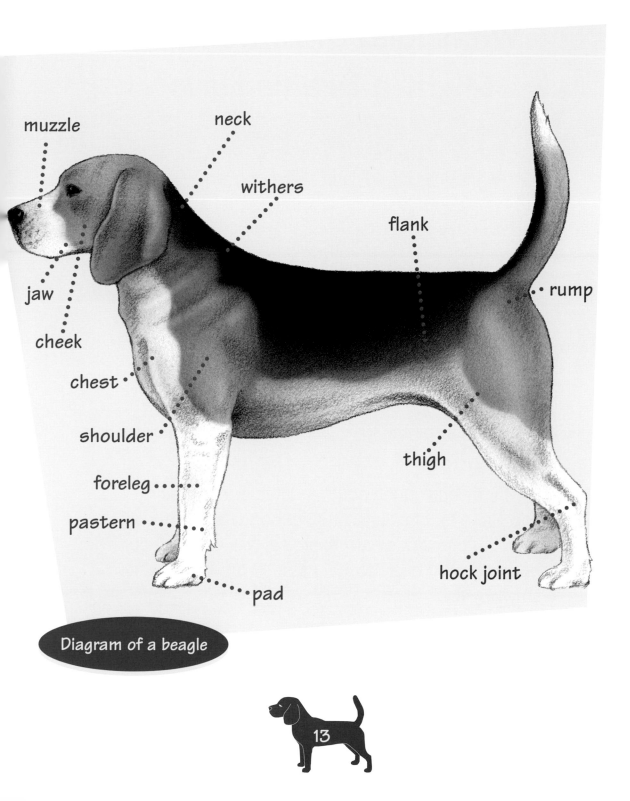

muzzle

neck

withers

flank

jaw

cheek

chest

shoulder

foreleg

pastern

thigh

rump

hock joint

pad

Diagram of a beagle

13

What Kind of Personality Might a Beagle Have?

Beagles are generally loyal, lovable dogs, which makes them a popular choice among families. They are considered to be good with children and are usually easy to train.

Beagles are pack animals, so they like to be around other dogs and people. They are also very curious. They will follow an unusual smell or sight to find out what it is.

Though beagles are generally easygoing dogs, they also can be quite stubborn. Because of this, it is very important to train your beagle from an early age so it learns to obey you.

Puppy and young adult beagles are energetic and like a lot of exercise. Older beagles can become lazy, but they need daily exercise, too. Getting your dog into good exercise habits early on will help it to stay healthy.

Beagles are lovable family pets.

15

Is a Beagle
the Dog for You?

Owning a dog is a big responsibility. Before you get a dog, you need to make sure that you and your family members have enough time and resources to properly care for it.

Though beagles are lovable dogs, they are not the right breed for everyone. All dogs need to get regular exercise, but beagles are very energetic and need to be taken for a long walk or a run at least once a day. They also like to be around people. If your family is away from home often, your beagle will be very lonely. Beagles are not usually noisy, but if they are left alone for long periods, they will start to bay (make a low howling sound).

If you plan to let your dog out in a yard by itself, you must have a fenced yard. Beagles are very curious. If they hear, smell, or see something unusual, they will try to follow it.

16

Some beagles like to live with other pets.

What Should You Look for When Choosing a Beagle Puppy?

Before buying any puppy, you need to make sure that you are working with a good breeder. To find a good breeder, you can check a national or local dog club. Organizations like the American Kennel Club (AKC) have Web sites that provide information about what to look for in a breeder. (See page 64 for Web site listings.) You can also talk to a veterinarian or a beagle owner to get advice.

The best time to bring a puppy home is when it is between 8 and 12 weeks old. This allows the puppy enough time to gain health benefits from being around its mother and brothers and sisters. This time also allows the puppy to gain skills it will need for you to train it later.

Ask the breeder about the personalities of the different puppies to help you choose. Most importantly, trust your instincts. Choose a puppy that you and your family connect with.

Beagle puppies

Should You Get an Older Beagle Instead of a Puppy?

There are many reasons that people find they cannot care for a dog. Some of these reasons may include a lack of time or money. Fortunately, there are shelters that take in dogs that need homes. There are also rescue organizations for certain breeds that try to place abandoned dogs in new homes. Adopting an older dog from a shelter, rescue organization, or previous owner can save its life.

Getting an older dog can have many advantages. Because they are already house-trained, older dogs may be less work than puppies. Older dogs are also fully developed, so you can tell how big they are and what kind of personality they may have.

It is important to find out as much as you can about an older dog before adopting it. If the dog has been mistreated, it may have health or personality problems. A beagle that has been mistreated may be shy, scared, or nervous. Beagles are unlikely to be mean.

Adopting a dog from a shelter can be a rewarding experience.

What Does a Beagle Eat?

Beagles take food very seriously. You should never interrupt a beagle—or any other dog—when it is eating. Even a gentle, well-trained dog may get upset at having its meal disturbed.

Like people, dogs need a healthful diet with different nutrients (nourishing substances). But dogs and people are different and should not eat the same food. Some human foods, such as chocolate, grapes and raisins, soft drinks, and sugarless candies, are poisonous to dogs and can even kill them.

If you are feeding your beagle high-quality food, it will probably only need one or two cups of food a day. This is not very much for such an active dog. Because beagles like to eat, you have to be careful not to overfeed them. Your veterinarian should be able to recommend the right food for your beagle.

When you first bring your puppy home, you should keep feeding it the same food that it is used to eating, on the same schedule. After the first few weeks, your family can discuss changing the routine or food with your veterinarian.

A beagle eating

23

Where Should a Beagle Sleep?

Most dog experts recommend that owners give their dog its own space to rest and sleep. Your family can purchase a small crate with bedding or a dog bed for your beagle. You should make sure that any soft bedding is washable. This will help to protect your dog from fleas.

If you buy a crate that is approved for airline travel, you can use the same crate when traveling by plane or car. Having its own familiar space will make your dog feel more comfortable when traveling.

Some people enjoy having a dog sleep on their bed, but you should ask an adult before letting your beagle sleep with you. It may seem like a fun idea, but some dogs aren't good sleeping companions. If your dog gets into the habit of sleeping with you, it will be very difficult to get him or her to stop.

A sleepy beagle

25

How Do You Groom a Beagle?

Beagles have a rough, medium-length coat. Under this fur is a fine undercoat made up of softer fur. The coat needs brushing once or twice a week, more often when the dog is shedding. Female beagles shed their coat after each season, and males shed it once a year. Beagles seldom need to be bathed, and then only when they're dirty or when they smell bad.

Those adorable, droopy ears can be a problem for beagles. They may get ear mites or infections. Ear mites are hard to see with just your eye. If you can see them, they will look like small white dots. Usually, you will see a dry, black discharge that looks a little like coffee grounds. You should check your beagle's ears every week for the discharge or white dots. Other symptoms of ear trouble are constant head shaking or ear scratching. If you think your dog has mites or an infection, call your veterinarian as soon as possible.

A beagle's toenails need to be checked frequently. You will need to have an adult trim your dog's toenails every week or two. The less active your dog is, the more often it will need its nails trimmed.

26

Bathing a beagle

What About Training a Beagle?

Training a beagle requires patience. Though they are smart and like to please people, beagles can be stubborn and get bored easily. It is important that dog owners get advice, or even take classes, on how to properly train their dog.

It is best to start researching how to train your dog before it comes home. You may also want to talk to people who own an older beagle to get advice on what sorts of problems may occur. Because beagles are hunting dogs, they have certain behaviors, such as rolling in stinky piles, which you or your parents may not enjoy.

Training a beagle will help it to learn how to behave and how to communicate. It is very important that you begin training your dog when it is a puppy so that it does not form bad habits.

You can get help training your dog from an expert at a dog obedience school. To find out about dog obedience schools in your area, check with your veterinarian or a local dog organization.

A beagle learning tricks

What Kinds of Exercise or Play Are Needed?

Young beagles are lively and energetic. They are bred to follow animals for long distances, so they like to take long walks and to run. It is very important that your beagle gets plenty of exercise every day to keep it happy and healthy.

Exercising with your beagle doesn't have to be a chore. It can be much fun. Beagles can be trained to do tricks or to play catch, and they will enjoy that exercise.

If your family likes to run or jog, you can take your beagle running. However, it is important not to over-exercise a young dog. A puppy's skeleton is still developing. If your beagle is under 18 months old, you should not run for more than half a mile (0.8 kilometers). Once your beagle is over 18 months old, you can start to add half a mile every week. In addition, you should wait to run with your beagle until it is properly trained on a leash.

Young beagles
love to play.

Do Beagles Like Water?

While beagles and many other hounds can swim, they do not always like to do so. For some hounds, such as basset hounds, swimming is actually very difficult. These short, stout dogs do not have bodies made for swimming.

Some breeds of hounds were bred to hunt animals that live in the water. Otterhounds were bred to hunt otters. These dogs love the water and are good swimmers.

Beagles generally do not like to swim—or get a bath. However, you will likely have to give your beagle a bath from time to time. When doing so, be sure to pay special attention to cleaning its ears, but don't pour water directly into the ears. This can cause an ear infection. Always make sure to dry off your dog well after a bath.

If your family or neighbors have a swimming pool, be sure to keep an eye on your dog when it plays near it. If the dog falls into the pool, it may have trouble finding its way out, even if it's a good swimmer.

Beagles do not usually like water.

Should You Breed Your Beagle?

There are many pets in the world that don't have homes. It is estimated that up to 8 million dogs and cats go into shelters in the United States every year, and only about half find homes. Because of this, most people should not breed their dogs, however fun it sounds to have cute puppies around.

If you get a rescue dog, you may be asked to make sure the dog cannot have puppies. A good breeder may ask you to do the same. People often buy purebred dogs to create more dogs of the breed. If this is not your plan, you should have your dog spayed or neutered. (A vet spays a female dog and neuters a male dog.) Your vet will perform a simple operation that will prevent unwanted puppies.

A beagle mother and her puppies

Are There Special Organizations for Beagle Owners?

People who love dogs love to talk and share information about dogs. There are many local, national, and international groups for dog owners. There are also many groups just for beagle owners, such as the National Beagle Club of America.

On page 64 of this book, you will see some suggestions for Web sites where you can find organizations for beagle owners. Remember, you should never give out personal information online, including your name, address, or phone number. Before joining a group that costs money, be sure to discuss it with a parent or other responsible adult.

Dog organizations can be a good place to get recommendations on everything from breeders to obedience information. The American Kennel Club, the Canadian Kennel Club, the Kennel Club in the United Kingdom, and the Australian National Kennel Council are just a few organizations that sponsor programs and events for all recognized dog breeds, including beagles.

A beagle gathering

How Do Hounds Help People?

Beagles and other hounds have an excellent sense of smell, hearing, and vision, so they are often used in police and detective work. Governments use beagles to sniff out fruits, meat, and vegetables that should not be brought between countries. Beagles are also used to detect termites. (Termites are wood-burrowing insects that can cause great damage to buildings.)

In many countries, bloodhounds, a large hunting dog, and other hounds are used to help find missing people. Proof provided by bloodhounds can be used in almost any court of law.

Because they are generally friendly and small, beagles can be used as therapy dogs. Therapy dogs are dogs that have been trained to provide comfort to people. Sometimes people in hospitals or nursing homes feel sad or lonely. Scientists have found that having time with a pet can help people feel better.

A beagle sniffing luggage

What Are Some Other Hound Breeds?

Dog organizations use words like *hound* to classify, or group, dogs. The terms help people know a little bit about the dog. They also help people group dogs together at dog shows.

Hounds are sometimes divided into sight hounds and scent hounds. These terms refer to what sense the dog uses to hunt. Sight hounds have excellent vision. Scent hounds have an excellent sense of smell.

The American Kennel Club lists 23 different breeds of hounds. Some popular examples of hounds are dachshunds, Rhodesian ridgebacks, basset hounds, greyhounds, and whippets. These dogs come from all over the world and were originally bred for different kinds of hunting. Dog organizations from different countries have similar groupings.

On the following pages, you can learn more about several different breeds of hounds.

Irish wolfhounds are one of the largest hound breeds.

What Is a Basset Hound?

Basset hounds are instantly recognizable for their heavy bodies, short legs, and sad eyes. Most basset hounds are black, white, and tan or red and white. A typical basset hound stands from 12 to 14 inches (30 to 36 centimeters) high, and weighs from 45 to 60 pounds (20 to 27 kilograms).

Basset hounds were originally bred in France in the 1600's. The word *basset* comes from the French word meaning "low." Because they are low to the ground, they were used to hunt rabbits and other small animals that are hunted by people on foot. Today, basset hounds are still used for hunting rabbits.

Basset hounds are known to be sweet and gentle. Like most hounds, they have a short coat of fur and do not require a lot of grooming. They can be excellent companions. But, because they love to follow scents or odors, they can be difficult to take on walks. A slow walk can turn into a fast run if your basset hound starts chasing after a new smell.

No other dog looks quite like a basset hound.

What Is a Bloodhound?

Bloodhounds are large hounds. They weigh from 80 to 110 pounds (36 to 50 kilograms). They have black and tan, red and tan, or yellowish-brown coats. Like basset hounds, bloodhounds have long, droopy ears. They also have a wrinkled face.

People often use the word *bloodhound* to describe a person who refuses to give up on solving a mystery. This is because bloodhounds are known for their ability to follow a scent for long distances. Bloodhounds have been using their sense of smell to hunt for about 2,000 years. They are mentioned in an ancient Roman study on animals written in the A.D. 200's.

The modern form of a bloodhound developed in England in the 1100's. The breed continued to develop and reached its current form in the United States.

Bloodhounds are often used in police work. They are very affectionate dogs, but they can be stubborn and may act hurt when you try to correct their behavior.

Bloodhounds are often described as looking like they're wearing a baggy suit.

What Is a Dachshund?

Sometimes known as "hot dogs" for their long, tubelike bodies, dachshunds *(DAHKS hunds)* are an adorable breed of hound. These small dogs were originally bred in Germany to hunt badgers and dig into their burrows. (The word *dachshund* means "badger dog" in German.)

Dachshunds have a glossy coat that is reddish, black, cream, tan, brown, or gray. The coat may be all one color, one color with patches of another color, spotted, or striped. Many dachshunds have short, smooth hair, but there are also long-haired and wire-haired varieties. Standard dachshunds usually weigh between 16 and 32 pounds (7.25 and 14.5 kilograms). Though dachshunds are already small, they also come in a miniature variety.

Dachshunds are brave, friendly, playful dogs that make excellent family pets. They are also surprisingly good watchdogs. However, they can have a stubborn streak and may not be able to fit into new situations unless properly trained.

Dachshunds are often called "hot dogs" because of their long, narrow shape.

What Is a Rhodesian Ridgeback?

The Rhodesian *(roh DEE zhuhn)* ridgeback is a large, strong hound from Africa that was originally bred to protect families and hunt lions. This dog is sometimes called the "African lion hound."

In the 1600's, many Europeans moved to South Africa with such dogs as great danes, mastiffs, and other large working dogs. The European immigrants bred the dogs they brought with them with native African dogs. These dogs were later brought to Rhodesia (modern-day Zimbabwe) and further bred to eventually become Rhodesian ridgebacks.

Like the African dogs they were bred from, Rhodesian ridgebacks have a ridge of fur along their spine that grows in the opposite direction of the rest of their fur. They grow to between 24 and 27 inches (61 and 68.5 centimeters) tall at the shoulder and weigh between 70 and 85 pounds (31.75 and 38.5 kilograms).

Most Rhodesian ridgebacks love to be around people and are considered good family dogs. However, they love to run and need lots of exercise every day.

Rhodesian ridgebacks are known for their distinct "ridge" of fur along the spine.

What Is an Afghan Hound?

The Afghan hound is a tall, slender dog with long ears, large feet, and a heavy coat of long, silky hair that has a fine texture. The coat can be many different colors. Afghan hounds stand about 27 inches (69 centimeters) tall at the shoulder and weigh about 50 to 60 pounds (23 to 27 kilograms).

Afghan hounds are known for their speed and liveliness. They are sight hounds, so they have amazing vision. For this very reason, it is not recommended that Afghan hound owners ever let their dog off the leash when it's in an open outdoor area.

No one knows exactly where or when the Afghan hound originated. The breed has been used for hunting gazelles, hares, and snow leopards in Afghanistan for hundreds of years.

The Afghan hound has a dignified appearance, moving with its head and tail held high. Because of this, Afghan hounds are considered excellent show dogs. They can also make great family pets, though they can be shy or unfriendly around strangers.

An Afghan hound

51

What Is a Dog Show Like?

Dog shows have become very popular in recent years. They are a way for pet owners to display their dog and to show how well trained it is.

Most dog shows are run by such organizations as the American Kennel Club, Australian National Kennel Council, Canadian Kennel Club, and New Zealand Kennel Club. These groups have certain rules about how a dog must appear and behave. Many of these groups allow young people to participate in junior divisions of the show.

Different dogs are judged on different characteristics. Hounds are judged on their tracking or chasing ability. They are also expected to stay cheerful while performing tasks.

Whether or not a dog is considered show quality has nothing to do with how good a dog it is, or what kind of pet it will make.

A beagle competes at a dog show.

Are There Dangers to Dogs Around the Home?

In some ways, dogs, especially puppies, are like small children. They tend to want to chew and bite new and unfamiliar items. Puppies have to be trained not to chew things like electrical cords and shoes.

Dogs should only chew specially made dog toys. These toys are designed for a dog's strong teeth. If a dog chews on a baby toy, the toy may break into small pieces. This could choke the dog.

Cleaning supplies and poisons bought to get rid of mice or bugs can quickly poison small dogs, such as beagles and dachshunds. You should always make sure to keep poisons and medicines in a locked cabinet. Small dogs can also easily jump through small openings in windows. If possible, open windows from the top; if not, make sure they are only open a few inches or centimeters.

54

A beagle at home

What Are Some Common Signs of Illness?

The most common health problems with beagles include allergies, eye problems, and epilepsy (a brain disorder). In addition, beagles sometimes have very sensitive stomachs and can be made sick by eating the wrong food. They also occasionally have problems with their hips.

If beagles do not get enough exercise, they can become obese. This creates more health problems.

Because dogs can't tell us how they feel, it is important to observe your pet closely so you know when something is wrong. If your beagle's behavior seems to change in any way, it is best to have a family member call the vet to see if your dog may be sick. Some general symptoms of illness in dogs include a lack of appetite, tiredness, vomiting, diarrhea, frequent urination, wheezing or heavy panting, and weakness.

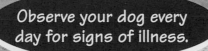

Observe your dog every day for signs of illness.

What Routine Veterinary Care Is Needed?

Like people, dogs need regular medical checkups to stay healthy. Finding a good veterinarian is an essential first step to becoming a dog owner.

When your family takes your dog to the vet, he or she will perform a physical exam, checking the dog for possible problems. Your dog will also need regular vaccinations, or shots. These shots help to protect your dog from getting certain illnesses. Some dog illnesses can be dangerous to people. Depending on where you live, the law may require you to give your dog certain vaccinations, and to keep a record of the shots.

The vet may give your dog medicine to keep it free of parasites, such as worms, fleas, ticks, and ear mites. These parasites can make your dog sick or uncomfortable.

Experts say that a dog should have a complete checkup with a vet every year.

Regular veterinary care is important for your dog.

What Are Your Responsibilities as an Owner?

A responsibility is something you are required to do. You may already have certain responsibilities, such as taking care of a younger sibling, getting good grades, or keeping your room clean.

Owning a dog gives you more responsibilities. If you choose to get a dog, you must honor those responsibilities, even if you are sick, tired, or just bored. Some of the responsibilities of owning a dog include feeding, grooming, and caring for it. You also have a responsibility to clean up after your dog, and to make sure it does not harm or bother other people.

Owning a dog is a big responsibility, but the friendship you and your dog will share may bring you great joy.

Beagles need much love and companionship.

Hound Fun Facts

→ The Norwegian lundehund is the rarest dog in the world. There are only between 1,500 and 2,000 lundehunds worldwide. These dogs have six toes on each foot and were originally bred to hunt puffins. Most dogs have 42 teeth, but lundehunds have only 40.

→ The most famous beagle of all is Snoopy from "Peanuts." The cartoons of this supper-loving beagle have been translated into 21 different languages.

→ Greyhounds can run up to 40 miles per hour (64 kilometers per hour).

→ The first British hounds were brought to the American Colonies in 1650 by the governor of Maryland, Robert Brooke.

→ The ship that Charles Darwin took on his voyages to make his great discoveries was known as the H.M.S. *Beagle.* In 2003, the European Space Agency sent Beagle 2, named for this ship, to explore Mars.

Glossary

allergy A reaction, or change, caused by something that would not ordinarily be harmful to human beings, such as animal fur or dust.

ancestor An animal from which another animal is directly descended. Usually, *ancestor* is used to refer to an animal more removed than a parent or grandparent.

breed To produce animals by carefully selecting and mating them for certain traits. Also, a group of animals having the same type of ancestors.

breeder A person who breeds animals.

burrow A hole dug in the ground by an animal for shelter. Also, to dig a hole in the ground.

groom To take care of an animal, for example, by combing, brushing, or trimming its coat.

neuter To operate on a male animal to make it unable to produce young.

pack A number of animals of the same kind hunting or living together. Also, a group of dogs kept together for hunting.

parasite An organism (living creature) that feeds on and lives on or in the body of another organism, often causing harm to the being on which it feeds.

purebred An animal whose parents are known to have both belonged to one breed.

shed To throw off or lose hair, skin, fur, or other body covering.

spay To operate on a female animal to make it unable to have young.

trait A feature or characteristic particular to an animal or breed of animals.

Index <small>(**Boldface** indicates a photo, map, or illustration.)</small>

For more information about beagles and other hounds, try these resources:

Books:

The Beagle Handbook by Dan Rice (Barrons, 2000)

Beagles by Susan Heinrichs Gray (Child's World, 2008)

The Complete Dog Book for Kids by the American Kennel Club (Howell Book House, 1996)

Superpuppy: How to Choose, Raise, and Train the Best Possible Dog for You by Jill and Daniel Manus Pinkwater (Clarion Books, 2002)

Web sites:

American Kennel Club
http://www.akc.org

Australian National Kennel Council
http://www.ankc.org.au/home/default.asp

The Canadian Kennel Club
http://www.ckc.ca/en/

The Kennel Club
http://www.thekennelclub.org.uk/

National Beagle Club of America
http://clubs.akc.org/NBC

Humane Society of the United States
http://www.hsus.org

The Hunting Dog: Hound Dogs
http://www.the-hunting-dog.com/hound-dogs.html

Dog Classification

Scientists classify animals by placing them into groups. The animal kingdom is a group that contains all the world's animals. Phylum, class, order, and family are smaller groups. Each phylum contains many classes. A class contains orders, an order contains families, and a family contains genuses. One or more species belong to each genus. Each species has its own scientific name. Here is how the animals in this book fit into this system.

Animals with backbones and their relatives (Phylum Chordata)
Mammals (Class Mammalia)
Carnivores (Order Carnivora)

Dogs and their relatives (Family Canidae)

Domestic dog . . . . *Canis familiaris*